Shakespeare on Golf

"Such Time–Beguiling Sport"

Shakespeare on Golf

"Such Time-Beguiling Sport"

Compiled by David Goodnough

Introduction

Thanks to the Miramax Corporation and a Czech-English loafer by the name of Tom Stoppard the public has been sold on the idea that William Shakespeare was a great lover. Well, the boys down at the Mermaid Tavern would have had something to say about that! For not only was Will, as he called himself (see *Sonnet CXXXVI*), a lousy lover (read those sonnets carefully), but, more to the point, he was also a lousy golfer. How does one relate to the other, you might ask? Because it's impossible to be a great lover if you're a lousy golfer, and vice versa. A man who is off his game simply cannot concentrate on anything but that one horrible fact. Who has time for sweet words lisped into shell-like ears or for paying those important little attentions when one is three-putting greens and missing fairways with his tee shots? Conversely, if a golfer's game is going reasonably well, "he capers, he dances, he has eyes of youth, he writes verses, he speaks holidays, he smells April and May" (*The Merry Wives of Windsor*, III.ii). In other words, he's ready to embark on a stupendous affair. Thus are great lovers made.

How do we know that Shakespeare was a lousy golfer? By internal evidence, of course. Does this sound to you like somebody who regularly shoots in the 80s or even the low 90s: "How weary, stale, flat, and unprofitable seem to me all the uses of this world" (*Hamlet*, I.ii)? Or, "Of comfort no man speak: Let's talk of graves, of worms, and epitaphs; Make dust our paper, and with rainy eyes Write sorrow on the bosom of the earth" (*King Richard III*, III.ii)? Come on. Here is a clear case of golfer's depression, probably brought on by a perfectly horrible day on the links. There are hundreds of other examples, but they are too disheartening to dwell on here. The man was clearly a duffer.

There is a subtext to the work of Shakespeare that scholars have virtually ignored. It has nothing to do with the heart in conflict with itself; or Man's relation to God, country, and the universe; or the Discovery of the Human, whatever that may mean (go ask Harold Bloom). It has to do with golf. Sometimes this subtext rises glaringly to the surface, as in that business where Great Birnham wood comes to Dunsinane hill. Significantly, this takes place in *Macbeth* ("the Scottish play," as superstitious actors call it) and its generally gloomy setting and darkness may have more to do with the origins of the Game than with any objective correlativity. Anyway, to a golfer, this rearrangement of whole bits of landscape is not as improbable as it may seem. Many golfers swear that after they have hit a screaming drive right down the middle, the damned fairway has *moved.* Our club's Oldest Member himself swears that on one of his drives a clump of trees several hundred feet from the fairway got up and moved right into the line of his ball. I believe him. Generally, though, Will kept his golf allusions concealed much more successfully than his sophomoric lubricity—but that's another matter.

In the pages that follow, I have tried to bring some of Will's golf subtext to light, and as a side-light to demonstrate once again the man's uncanny precognition. I believe that he could actually see into the future and to give "to airy nothing A local habitation and a name" (*A Midsummer Night's Dream*, V.i). Too bad that that "airy nothing" probably could have been used just as well to describe his golf swing.

Tee Off!

Aces, eagles, and birdies

We are such stuff
As dreams are made on.

—*The Tempest,* IV.i

Affection for the pro game

Their love
Lies in their purses.

—*King Richard II,* II.ii

Aging pros

We'll draw cuts for the Senior.

—*The Comedy of Errors,* V.i

Amateur champion joins the Tour

His promises were, as he then was, mighty;
But his performance, as he is now, nothing.

—*King Henry VIII,* IV.ii

Amateur exempted to play in the Masters

—A Midsummer Night's Dream

Amateur taking part in first pro-am

Against ill chances men are very merry,
But heaviness foreruns the good event.

—King Henry IV, Part II, IV.ii

Amateurs in open and pro-am tournaments

They did battery to the spheres intend;
Sometimes diverted their poor balls are ty'd
To the orb'd earth; sometimes they do extend
To view right on.

—A Lover's Complaint

Another Spanish Golfer joins the Tour

I cannot tell what the dickens his name is.

—The Merry Wives of Windsor, III.ii

FAWNING FIRST-TIMER AT AUGUSTA NATIONAL

Most potent, grave, and reverend signiors,
My very noble and approv'd good Masters.

—*Othello*, I.iii

Anxious early tournament finishers

To reel the streets at noon, and stand the buffet
With knaves that smell of sweat.

—*Antony and Cleopatra,* I.iv

Arnold Palmer, Gary Player, Jack Nicklaus, et al.

Though I look old, yet I am strong and lusty.

—*As You Like It,* II.iii

Arnold Palmer's gallery

'Tis a brave army,
And full of purpose.

—*Antony and Cleopatra,* IV.iii

August fairways

Why, these balls bound; there's noise in it.—
'Tis hard.

—*All's Well That Ends Well,* II.iii

Augusta National official to upstart rookie

Am I the Master here, or you? go to.

—*Romeo and Juliet,* I.v

Ball ending up in a divot

An odious damned lie;
Upon my soul, a lie, a wicked lie.

—*Othello,* V.ii

Beer endorsement

Make my image but an alehouse sign.

—*King Henry VI, Part II,* III.ii

Ben Hogan

We that are young
Shall never see so much, nor live so long.

—*King Lear,* V.iii

Big-money tournament win

A victory is twice itself when the achiever brings
home full numbers

—*Much Ado About Nothing,* I.i.

Bitter out-of-the-money player

They laugh that win.

—*Othello,* IV.i

Blast from bunker into the cup

Sweet are the uses of adversity.

—*As You Like It,* II.i

Caddie master

I will use them according to their desert.

—*Hamlet,* II.ii

Caddie's considered opinion

Uneven is the course; I like it not.

—*Romeo and Juliet,* IV.i

Calling it quits

When from high-most pitch, with weary car,
Like feeble age, he reeleth from the day.

—*Sonnet VII*

Casey Martin upon receiving his Tour card

Why, now you have done me right.

—*King Henry IV, Part II,* V.iii

Chance for first win in a major

If it be now, 'tis not to come; if it be not to come, it will be now; if it be not now, yet it will come: the readiness is all.

—*Hamlet,* V.ii

Clincher in a tournament invitation

Hold, there's expenses for thee.

—*Twelfth Night,* III.i

Clothing logos

We are advertis'd by our loving friends.

—*King Henry VI, Part III,* V.iii

Club bitcher

Then give me leave; for losers will have leave
To ease their stomachs with their bitter tongues.

—*Titus Andronicus,* III.i

Club clown

I will be strange, stout, in yellow stockings, and cross-gartered, even with the swiftness of putting on.

—*Twelfth Night,* II.v

Club hypochondriac

I am too much i' the sun.

—*Hamlet,* I.ii

Club pro joins the Tour

Better at home, if "would I might" were
"may."—
But to the sport abroad

—*Troilus and Cressida,* I.i

Club pro who has been invited to play in a major

There's not a man I meet but doth salute me
As if I were their well-acquainted friend;
And every one doth call me by my name.
Some tender money to me; some invite me;
Some other give thanks for kindnesses;
Some offer me commodities to buy.

—*The Comedy of Errors,* IV.iii

Club tournament director—I

Ay me, poor man, how pale and wan he looks!

—*The Comedy of Errors,* IV.iv

Club tournament director—II

This week he hath been heavy, sour, sad,
And much different from the man he was.

—*The Comedy of Errors,* V.i

Club Whiner

I ne'er had worse luck in my life.

—*All's Well That Ends Well,* II.ii

Clubhouse bar closed during tournament

O vile,
Intolerable, not to be endured!

—*The Taming of the Shrew,* V.ii

Clubhouse bar open only to members during tournament

A thousand times more fair, ten thousand
times more rich.

—*The Merchant of Venice,* III.ii

Clubhouse porch critics

Look you yonder, do you see? look you there:
there's no jesting; there's no laying on, tak't off
who will, as they say: there be hacks!

—*Troilus and Cressida,* I.ii

Clubhouse scoreboard

Who loses and who wins; who's in, who's out.

—*King Lear,* V.iii

Club-thrower calms himself

I will not stir, nor wince, nor speak a word,
Nor look upon the iron angerly.

—*King John,* IV.i

Colin Montgomerie to American fans

Here. Why dost thou spit at me?

—*King Richard III,* I.ii

Comeback pro with a drug problem

A little pot and soon hot.

—*The Taming of the Shrew,* IV.i

Competent but unspectacular pro

Nothing comes amiss, so money comes withal.

—*The Taming of the Shrew,* I.ii

Competing pros watching Tiger Woods tee off

Alas, how fiery and sharp he looks!

—*The Comedy of Errors,* IV.iv

Conceited professional

And all the courses of my life do show
I am not in the roll of common men.

—*Henry IV, Part I,* III.i

Confident co-leader going into final round

I'll strive, with troubled thoughts, to take a nap,
Lest leaden slumber peise me down to-morrow,
When I should mount with wings of victory.

—*King Richard III,* V.iii

Confident home pro

I know my course.

—*Hamlet,* II.ii

Confident pro entering final round

Doubt not of the day,
And that once gotten, doubt not of large pay.

—*King Henry VI, Part III,* IV.vii

Confident pro with a strong short game

Up and down, up and down,
I will lead them up and down.

—*A Midsummer Night's Dream,* III.ii

Confident wedge hitter

Here, in the sands,
Thee I'll rake up.

—*King Lear,* IV.vi

Consoling thought before playoff round

The selfsame heaven
That frown on me looks sadly upon him.

—*King Richard III,* V.iii

Correcting a natural swing

And thus the native hue of resolution
Is sicklied o'er with the pale cast of thought.

—*Hamlet,* III.i

Course closed for the season

Now is the winter of our discontent.

—*King Richard III,* I.i

Course designer's motto

To cross the curious workmanship of nature,
To mingle beauty with infirmities,
And pure perfection with impure defeature;
Making it subject to the tyranny
Of mad mischances and much misery.

—*Venus and Adonis,* ll. 734-38

Course manager

O, how full of briars is this working-day world!

—*As You Like It,* I.iii

Course opened for the season

If I may trust the flattering eye of sleep,
My dreams presage some joyful news at hand;
My bosom's lord sits lightly on his throne;
And all this day an unaccostum'd spirit
Lifts me above the ground with cheerful thoughts.

—*Romeo and Juliet,* V.i

Critical golf writers

Poor breathing orators of miseries!
Let them have scope.

—*King Richard III,* IV.iv

GOING FOR ONE UNDER

Hillo, ho, ho, boy! come bird, come.

—*Hamlet,* I.v

Critical press coverage

Why should calamity be full of words?

—*King Richard III,* IV.iv

David Duval

Seldom he smiles, and smiles in such a sort
As if he mocked himself, and scorn'd his spirit
That could be moved to smile at anything.

—*Julius Caesar,* I.ii

Davis III just misses another major

Love's Labour's Lost

Defensive minor tournament director

We cannot all be Masters.

—*Measure for Measure,* V.i

Disastrous round

The worst is not,
So long as we can say, "This is the worst,"

—*King Lear,* IV.i

Doubtful of caddie's advice

Be sure of it; give me the ocular proof.

—*Othello,* III.iii

Drought effect

The ground, indeed, is tawny.

—*The Tempest,* II.i

Duffer finally breaks 100

It is upon record, or else reported
Successfully from age to age?

—*King Richard III,* III.i

Dunlace Course, Northern Ireland, 5th hole

This castle hath a pleasant seat.

—*Macbeth,* I.vi

Early leader learns that late starters are tearing up the course

If there be more, more woeful, hold it in;
For I am almost ready to dissolve,
Hearing of this.

—*King Lear,* V.iii

Early morning finish

O most lame and impotent conclusion.!

—*Othello,* I.i

Early morning start

This morning, like the spirit of youth
That means to be of note, begins betimes.

—*Antony and Cleopatra,* IV.iv

Early morning starters after 18 holes

Come, Come, away!
The sun is high, and we outwear the day.

—*King Henry V,* IV.ii

Early morning tee-off time—I

To business that we love we rise betime,
And go to't with delight.

—*Antony and Cleopatra,* IV.iv

Early morning tee-off time—II

Would it were day!...
Will it never be morning?...
What a long night is this!...

Will it never be day?...
Would it were day!

—*King Henry V,* III.vii

Early season's drawback

The uncertain glory of an April day,
Which now shows all the beauty of the sun,
And by and by a cloud takes all away!

—*The Two Gentlemen of Verona,* I.iii

Effeminate club pest

Bid me discourse, I will enchant thine ear,
Or, like a fairy, trip upon the green,
Or, like a nymph, with long dishevell'd hair,
Dance on the sands, and yet no footing seen.

—*Venus and Adonis,* ll. 145-48

End of sponsor exemptions

'Tis a consummation
Devoutly to be wisht.

—*Hamlet,* III.i

Ensuring full press coverage

Gentlemen, prepare not to be gone;

We have a trifling foolish banquet towards.

—*Romeo and Juliet,* I.v

European team to 1999 Ryder Club gallery

Are you not ashamed
With this immodest clamorous outrage?

—*King Henry VI, Part II,* IV.i

Exempted amateur on Tour

Such unconstant starts are we like to have from him.

—*King Lear,* I.i

Extremely early morning star

Not to be abed before midnight is to be up betimes.

—*Twelfth Night,* II.iii

Extremely slow putter

God save the mark.

—*King Henry IV, Part I,* I.iii

SHOOTING AROUND A DOGLEG RIGHT

Slice, I say! pauca, pauca, pauca, slice!

—*The Merry Wives of Windsor,* I.i

Fair weather caddie

That sir which serves and seeks for gain,
And follows but for form,
Will pack when it begins to rain,
And leave thee in the storm.

—*King Lear,* II.iv

A few drinks at the clubhouse bar

Then shall we have a match.

—*All's Well That Ends Well,* V.iii

Finish of 1999 Ryder Cup matches

If this were played upon a stage now, I could condemn it as an improbable fiction

—*Twelfth Night,* III.iv

First round leader

Thus far our fortune keeps an upward course,
And we are graced with wreaths of victory.

—*King Henry VI, Part III,* V.iii

First round of the season

For this, be sure, tonight thou shalt have cramps.

—*The Tempest,* I.ii

First-time winner of a major, to manufacturers' reps

Come, woo me, woo me,
For I am in a holiday humour.

—*As You Like It,* IV.i

First women pro golfers

So you walk softly, and look sweetly, and say nothing.

—*Much Ado About Nothing,* II.i

5 iron

This is the short and the long of it.

—*The Merry Wives of Windsor,* II.ii

Five years on the tour without a win

What potions have I drunk of Syren tears,
Distill'd from limbecs foul as hell within,
Applying fears to hopes, and hopes to fears,
Still losing when I saw myself to win!
What wretched errors hath my heart committed,
Whilst it hath thought itself so blessed never!

—*Sonnet CXIX*

Forced to go back to Qualifying School

Men must endure
Their going hence, even as their coming hither.

—*King Lear,* V.ii

Fore!

Something wicked this way comes.

—*Macbeth,* IV.i

Forgiving skins partner

Come, come, come, come, give me your hand: what's
done cannot be undone.

—*Macbeth,* V.i

Fortunate out-of-bounds shots

These are gracious drops.

—*Julius Caesar,* II.ii

4 over on the front nine, 6 under on the back

So foul and fair a day I have not seen.

—*Macbeth,* I.iii

Fuzzy thinking when competing with Tiger Woods

But since he is better'd [said to be superior], we have
therefore odds.

—*Hamlet,* V.ii

Gallery dispersion

Now spurs the lated traveller apace
To gain the timely inn.

—*Macbeth,* III.iii

Gary McCord

I am not only witty in myself, but the cause
that wit is in other men.

—*King Henry IV, Part II,* I.i

Gary Player, from opponents' perspective

The black prince, sir, alias the prince of darkness,
alias the devil.

—*All's Well That Ends Well,* IV.v

Gary Player, from his fans' perspective

He has his health, and ampler strength indeed
Than most men have of his age.

—*The Winter's Tale,* IV.iii

Geese on fairway, delaying play

Oh hell! what have we here?

—*The Merchant of Venice,* II.vii

Gene Sarazen remembered

For the great swing and rudeness of his poise.

—*Troilus and Cressida,* I.iii

Generous but self-satisfied winner

I will praise any man that will praise me.

—*Antony and Cleopatra,* II.vi

Giving it all up to join the Tour

It is a life that I have desired: I will thrive.

—*The Merry Wives of Windsor,* I.iii

GOLF SIRENS

Come unto these yellow sands.

—*The Tempest,* I.ii

Going against the club pro

The harder match, the greater victory.

—*King Henry VI, Part III,* V.i

Goldbricking clubhouse personnel

Away! the gentles are at their game, and we will to our recreation.

—*Love's Labour's Lost,* IV.ii

Golf addiction

If I lose a scruple of this sport, let me be boiled to death with melancholy.

—*Twelfth Night,* II.v

Golf as a metaphor for life

Thus sometimes has the brightest day a cloud;
And after summer evermore succeeds
Barren winter, with his wrathful nipping cold:
So cares and joys abound, as seasons fleet.

—*King Henry VI,* II.iv

Golf as a restorative

And I can speak of the disturbances
That nature works, and of her cures; which doth
give me

A more content in course of true delight
Than to be thirsty after tottering honour,
Or tie my treasure up in silken bags,
To please the fool and death.

—*Pericles,* III.ii

Golf as therapy

'Twill do me good to walk.

—*Othello,* IV.iii

Golf carts not allowed

The game's afoot.

—*King Henry V,* III.i

The Golf Channel

This sport, well carried, shall be chronicled.

—*A Midsummer Night's Dream,* III.ii

Golf course in the boonies

It is too rough,
Too rude, too boisterous, and it pricks like a thorn.

—*Romeo and Juliet,* I.iv

Golf groupies

Daughters of the game.

—*Troilus and Cressida,* IV.v

Golf hustler

If thou dost play with him at any game,
Thou art sure to lose; and, of that natural luck,
He beats thee 'gainst the odds.

—*Antony and Cleopatra,* II.iii

Golf Register

What's past is prologue.

—*The Tempest,* II.i

Golfer matched against his wife

Whoever wins, on that side shall I lose:
Assured loss before the match be play'd.

—*King John,* III.i

Golfer to wife after a bad round

If you have tears, prepare to shed them now.

—*Julius Caesar,* III.ii

Golfer's wife

No, I will be the pattern of patience; I will say nothing.

—*King Lear,* III.ii

Golfing priest after missing two-footer

I prithee, give me leave to curse awhile.

—*King Henry VI, Part I,* V.iii

Good-looking LPGA leader

You should tread a course
Pretty and full of view.

—*Cymbeline,* III.iv

Good losing attitude

Praising what is lost
Makes the remembrance more dear.

—*All's Well That Ends Well,* V.iii

Good practice round

Why, so! then am I sure of victory.
Now therefore let us hence.

—*King Henry VI, Part III,* IV.i

Greens fee

Why so large a cost, having so short a lease?

—Sonnet CXLVI

Greg Norman

This chaos, when degree is suffocate,
Follows the choking.

—Troilus and Cressida, I.iii

Grooved swing

Custom hath made it in him a property of easiness.

—Hamlet, V.i

Hacker with serious temper problem

The vilest stroke,
That ever wall-eyed or staring rage
Presented to the tears of soft remorse.

—King John, IV.iii

Hall of Fame candidate

I have
Immortal longings in me.

—Antony and Cleopatra, V.ii

Hard fairways, soft greens

As You Like It

Hard-working pro

I have been in continual practice: I shall win at the odds.

—*Hamlet,* V.ii

Hazards of the Tour

Ruptures, catarrhs, loads o' gravel in the back,
lethargies,
cold palsies, raw eyes, dirt-rotten livers,
wheezing lungs,
bladders full of imposthume, sciaticas,
limekilns i'th'palms,
incurable bone ache.

—*Troilus and Cressida,* V.i

Hitting over the trees on a dogleg

O! that way madness lies; let me shun that;
No more of that.

—*King Lear,* III.iv

HARD-LUCK VETERAN OF THE TOUR

SCHOCH'97

A fellow that hath had losses.

—*Much Ado About Nothing*, IV.ii

Hitting straight for the pin

Why, 'tis a boisterous and a cruel style,
A style for challengers.

—*As You Like It,* IV.iii

Hitting to the right of a water hazard

Hook on, hook on.

—*King Henry IV, Part II,* II.i

Hole-in-one

O wonderful, wonderful, and most wonderful
wonderful! and yet again wonderful, and after that,
out of all whooping!

—*As You Like It,* III.ii

Homemade putter

An ill-favored thing, sir, but mine own.

—*As You Like It,* V.iv

Honest self-appraisal

Wrong hath but wrong, and blame the due of blame

—*King Richard III,* V.i

How's that again?

Good words are better than bad strokes.

—*Julius Caesar,* V.i

How to attract major players

Put money in thy purse.

—*Othello,* I.iii

Hyperactive golfer

What rounds, what bounds, what course, what stop
he makes!

—*A Lover's Complaint,* l. 109

I'll take it!

Near or far off, well won is still well shot.

—*King John,* I.i

Improving one's lie

Be bold to play, our sport is not in sight:
These blue-veined violets whereon we lean
Never can blab.

—*Venus and Adonis,* ll. 124-26

Inconsistent tee shots

Sometimes diverted their poor balls are ty'd
To the orb'd earth; sometimes they do extend
To view right on.

—*A Lover's Complaint*

Insisting on playing through

How poor are they that have no patience.

—*Othello,* II.iii

International golf architect

He'll shape his old course in a country new.

—*King Lear,* I.i

International Management Group (IMG)

O world! world! world! thus is the poor agent despised.

—*Troilus and Cressida,* V.x

Invited to take part in pro-am charity tournament

Now name the rest of the players.

—*A Midsummer Night's Dream,* I.ii

Jack Nicklaus—I

Why, man, he doth bestride the narrow earth
Like a Colossus.

—*Julius Ceasar,* I.ii

Jack Nicklaus—II

Bear-like, I must fight the course.

—*Macbeth,* V.vii

Jean Van de Velde on the final round of the '99 British Open

O call back yesterday, bid time return!

—*King Richard II,* II.iii

John Daly

That quaffing and drinking will undo you.

—*Twelfth Night,* I.iii

Keeping cool while looking into a bunker

I see the play so lies.

—*The Winter's Tale,* IV.iii

Kindly caddie to beginning golfer

I'll lead you about a round,
Through bog, through bush, through brake,
through briar.

—*A Midsummer Night's Dream,* III.i

Last finisher holes out

Now spurs the lated traveller apace
To gain the timely inn.

—*Macbeth,* III.iii

Last year's Masters winner

Uneasy lies the head that wears a crown.

—*King Henry IV, Part II,* III.i

Lazy starter

Will you go see the order of the course?

—*Julius Caesar,* I.ii

Lazy tour veteran

If all the year were playing holidays,
To sport would be as tedious as work.

—*King Henry IV, Part I,* I.ii

Lining up a putt

Measure for Measure

Listing of top PGA money winners

This news is old enough, yet it is every day's news.

—*Measure for Measure,* III.ii

Local qualifying rounds for U.S. Open

Why this is very midsummer madness.

—*Twelfth Night,* III.iv

Locker room blues

And do not drop in for an after-loss:
Ah! do not, when my heart hath scap'd this
sorrow,
Come in the rearward of a conquer'd woe;
Give not a windy night a rainy morrow,
To linger out a purpos'd overthrow.

—*Sonnet XC*

Locker room prayer group

Heaven prosper our sport!

—*The Merry Wives of Windsor,* V.ii

Locker room replay

For it comes to pass oft, that a terrible oath, with a swaggering accident sharply twang'd off, gives manhood more approbation than ever proof itself would have earn'd him.

—*Twelfth Night,* III.iv

Long putt over a ridge

O, break! O, break!

—*Antony and Cleopatra,* V.ii

Long-shafted putter as a cure for yips

Diseases desperate grown
By desperate appliances are relieved,
Or not at all.

—*Hamlet,* IV.iii

Looking for an explanation after missing the cut

Or else 'twere hard luck, being in so preposterous estate as we are.

—*Winter's Tale,* V.ii

Losing cumulative skins partners

Let us seek out some desolate shade, and there
Weep our sad bosoms empty.

—*Macbeth,* IV.iii

Lost ball

'Tis neither here nor there.

Othello, IV.iii

LPGA Tour members

And have not we affections,
Desires for sport, and frailty, as men have?

—*Othello,* IV.iii

Luck of the draw

Half won is match well made; match, and well make it.

—*All's Well That Ends Well,* IV.iii

Lucky to make the Buy.com (formerly Nike, formerly Ben Hogan) Tour

The play's the thing.

—*Hamlet,* II.ii

Made the cut

O most courageous day! O most happy hour!

—*A Midsummer Night's Dream,* IV.ii

Major winner submitting to the media

Who is it in the press that calls on me?
I hear a tongue shriller than all the music.

—*Julius Caesar,* I.ii

Major winner's overdemonstrative wife

I will rob Tellus [earth] of her weed,
To strew thy green with flowers.

—*Pericles,* IV.i

Mary Queen of Scots on golf

Sport royal, I warrant you.

—*Twelfth Night,* II.iii

Masters winner trying on green blazer

You won it, wore it, kept it, gave it me.

—*King Henry IV, Part II,* IV.iv

Meeting of the Rules Committee

O! there has been much throwing about of brains.

—*Hamlet,* II.ii

Michael Murphy's *Golf in the Kingdom*

Find out moonshine, find out moonshine.

—*A Midsummer Night's Dream,* III.i

Missed a two-footer

The destinies will curse thee for this stroke.

—*Venus and Adonis,* l. 946

Missed the cut—I

O woe! O woeful, woeful, woeful day!
Most lamentable day, most woeful day,
That ever, ever, I did yet behold!

—*Romeo and Juliet,* IV.v

Missed the cut—II

I will see what physic the tavern affords.

—*King Henry VI, Part I,* III.i

QUALIFYING ROUND

This was the most unkindest cut of all.

—*Julius Caesar,* III.ii

Missed the cut—III

I am gone.

—*Cymbeline, I.i*

Missed putt for match

There let him stand, and rave.

—*Titus Andronicus,* V.iii

Missing final putt that would have forced a playoff

And after that, he came, thus sad, away.

—*Julius Caesar,* I.ii

Mixed foursome

A summer's day will seem an hour but short,
Being wasted in such time-beguiling sport.

—*Venus and Adonis,* ll. 23-24

Mulligan

For this relief, much thanks.

—*Hamlet,* I.i

New club

Why, this hits right.

—*Timon of Athens,* III.i

New golf course approved by Planning Board

O joyful day!

—*King Henry IV, Part II,* V.iii

New golf course refused by Planning Board

Cry woe, destruction, ruin, loss, decay.

—*King Richard II,* III.ii

New tournament sponsor

A merchant of incomparable wealth.

—*The Taming of the Shrew,* IV.ii

New wraparound sunglasses

What a pair of spectacles are here!

—*Troilus and Cressida,* IV.iv

Newcomer to the senior tour

Is it not strange that desire should so many years
outlive performance.

—*King Henry IV, Part II,* II.iv

Next-to-last finisher

Not being the worst
Stands in some rank of praise.

—*King Lear,* II.v

Nice-guy winner of playoff

Give me thy hand: I'm sorry that I beat thee.

—*The Tempest,* III.ii

Nice try

This bird you aim'd at, through you hit her not;
Therefore a health to all that shot and mist.

—*The Taming of the Shrew,* V.ii

1999 U.S. Ryder Cup Team finish

They threw their caps
As they would hang them on the horns o' the moon
Shouting their emulation.

—*Coriolanus,* I.i

19th hole

'Tis the breathing time of day with me.

—*Hamlet,* V.ii

No pars, double and triple bogeys, and three lost balls

We have seen better days.

—*Timon of Athens,* IV.ii

Obligatory interviews with tournament finishers

Here will be an old abusing of God's patience and the king's English.

—*The Merry Wives of Windsor,* I.iv

Official marker

Have you scored me?

—*Othello,* IV.i

Old-fashioned fairway play

I should be still
Plucking the grass, to know where sits the wind.

—*The Merchant of Venice,* I.i

Old players versus modern

Then what they do in present,
Though less than yours in past, must o'ertop yours.

—*Troilus and Cressida,* III.iii

Optimistic non-qualifier

To be worst,
The lowest and most dejected thing of fortune,
Stands still in esperance, lives not in fear:
The lamentable change is from the best;
The worst returns to laughter.

—*King Lear,* IV.i

Out of the top ten, first round

'Tis but early days.

—*Troilus and Cressida,* IV.v

Overswing

Ho! now you strike like a blind man.

—*Much Ado About Nothing,* II.i

Overworked caddie

Most heavy day!

—*Antony and Cleopatra,* IV.xiv

Own worst enemy

And with those hands, that graspt the heaviest
club,
Subdue my worthiest self.

—*Antony and Cleopatra,* IV.xii

Partner's tee shots end up in creek

That is the true beginning of our end.

—*A Midsummer Night's Dream,* V.i

Party club's reception for visiting pros

We'll teach you to drink deep ere you depart.

—*Hamlet,* I.ii

Payne Stewart—I

Old fashions please me best.

—*The Taming of the Shrew,* II.i

Payne Stewart—II

He was a man, take him for all in all,
I shall not look on his like again.

—*Hamlet,* I.ii

Pebble Beach, 7th hole

What if it tempt you toward the flood, my lord,
Or to the dreadful summit of the cliff
That beetles o'er his base into the sea?

—*Hamlet,* I.iv

Penalized by referee for throwing his clubs

What wilt thou do, thou peevish officer?
Hast thou delight to see a wretched man
Do outrage and displeasure to himself?

—*The Comedy of Errors,* IV.iv

Personal statistics—Favorable

Thy gift, thy tables, are within my brain
Full character'd with lasting memory,
Which shall above that idle rank remain,
Beyond all date, even to eternity;
Or at least so long as brain and heart
Have faculty by nature to subsist;
Till each to raz'd oblivion yield his part
Of thee, thy record never can be miss'd.

—*Sonnet CXXII*

Personal statistics—Unfavorable

Thy registers and thee I both defy,

SELF SATISFIED PUTTER

This was well done, my bird.

—*The Tempest*, IV.i

Not wondering at the present nor the past;
For thy records and what we see do lie.

—*Sonnet CXXIII*

PGA leader's motive

To win this easy match play'd for a crown.

—*King John,* V.ii

PGA officials to Casey Martin

O, let me see thee walk.

—*The Taming of the Shrew,* II.i

PGA Qualifying School, first day

How many goodly creatures are there here!
How beauteous mankind is! O brave new
world,
That has such people in't.

—*The Tempest,* V.i

PGA Tour professionals

The wealthy curled darlings of our nation.

—*Othello,* I.i

PGA Winner's Cup

Have you beheld,
Or have you read or heard? or could you think?
Or do you almost think, although you see,
That you do see? could thought, without this object,
Form such another? This is the very top,
The height, the crest, or crest unto the crest.

—*King John,* IV.iii

Philosophical first-round trailer

The end crowns all;
And that old common arbitrator, Time,
Will one day end it.

—*Troilus and Cressida,* IV.v

Philosophical losing attitude

What's gone and what's past help
Should be past grief.

—*The Winter's Tale,* III.ii

Philosophical sudden-death playoff loser

Ay, that way goes the game.

—*A Midsummer Night's Dream,* III.ii

Pinehurst, North Carolina

The air breathes upon us here most sweetly.

—*The Tempest,* II.i

Play suspended because of rain

Delays have dangerous ends.

—*King Henry VI, Part I,* III.ii

Playoff loser

Let us seek out some desolate shade, and there weep our sad bosoms empty.

—*Macbeth,* IV.iii

Playoff loss

The expense of spirit in a waste of shame.

—*Sonnet CXXIX*

Poor finish

O most lame and impotent conclusion!

—*Othello,* II.i

Poor golfer who blames his long clubs

Shame not these woods,
By putting on the cunning of a carper.

—*Timon of Athens,* IV.iii

Poor loser

The game was ne'er so fair, and I am done.

—*Romeo and Juliet,* I.iv

Poor losing attitude

Oh! how bitter a thing it is to look into
happiness
through another man's eyes.

—*As You Like It,* V.ii

Poor pairing in a pro-am

There I have another bad match.

—*The Merchant of Venice,* III.i

Popular sports physician

Do with your injuries as seems you best.

—*Measure for Measure,* V.i

Post-tournament party

Mine, and most of our fortunes, to-night, shall be,—drunk to bed.

—*Anthony and Cleopatra,* I.ii

Posted pairings

What cunning match have you made with this jest of the drawer?

—*King Henry IV, Part I,* II.iv

Potential pro

To be or not to be; that is the question.

—*Hamlet,* III.i

Pro in retirement

When to the sessions of sweet silent thought
I summon up remembrance of things past.

—*Sonnet XXX*

Professional outlook

One business does command us all; mine
Is money.

—*Timon of Athens,* III.iv

Proud duffer who has finally broken 100

Is it upon record, or else reported
Successively from age to age?

—*King Richard III,* III.i

Prying sportswriter

The players cannot keep counsel; they'll tell all.

—*Hamlet,* III.ii

Public links

You know the course is common.

—*Measure for Measure,* IV.ii

Punch

Whereof a little
More than a little is by much too much.

—*King Henry IV, Part I,* III.ii

Qualified for the PGA Tour

Why, then the world's mine oyster.

—*The Merry Wives of Windsor,* II.ii

Questionable course book

Who hath measured the ground?

—*King Henry V,* III.vii

Reaction to editorials bemoaning decline of game

Then with the losers let it sympathise,
For nothing can seem foul to those that win.

—*King Henry IV, Part I,* V.i

Realistic assessment after receiving handicap

Past hope, past cure, past help!

—*Romeo and Juliet,* IV.i

Referee to player whose ball has lodged in a tree

How camest thou in this pickle?

—*The Tempest,* V.i

Reluctant Senior Tour member

For mine own part, I could be well content
To entertain the tag-end of my life
With quiet hours.

—*King Henry IV, Part I,* V.i

Ringer brought in for big-money Nassau

Under the colour of his usual game.

—*King Henry VI, Part III,* IV.v

Roll-in from 10 feet off the green

Zounds!

—*King John,* II.i

The Rules of Golf

This bookish theoric.

—*Othello,* I.i

Ryder Cup fan defends his fellows

And so far am I glad it so did sort,
As this their jangling I esteem a sport.

—*A Midsummer Night's Dream,* III.ii

Ryder Cup galleries—I

How earnestly they knock!

—*Troilus and Cressida,* IV.ii

QUESTIONABLE SCORE-CARDS

Then, gentle cheater, urge not my amiss,
Lest guilty of my faults thy sweet self prove.

—Sonnet CLI

Ryder Cup galleries—II

Mak'st thou this shame thy pastime?

—*King Lear,* II.iv

Ryder Cup team members

Why should our endeavor be so loved, and the performance so loathed?

—*Troilus and Cressida,* V.x

St. Andrews, Scotland

With hey, ho, the wind and the rain…
For the rain it raineth every day.

—*Twelfth Night,* V.i

Satisfying day at the club

And, being a winner, God give you good night.

—*The Taming of the Shrew,* V.ii

Satisfying round

Thy hand upon that match.

—*Troilus and Cressida,* IV.v

Saturday night anxiety

O, let the hours be short,
Till fields and blows and groans applaud
our sport!

—*King Henry IV, Part I,* I.iii

Scratch player

Here, there, and every where, he leaves and
takes;
Dexterity so obeying appetite,
That what he will he does; and does so much,
That proof is call'd impossibility.

—*Troilus and Cressida,* V.v

Searching for lost ball

Then thou shalt see the dew-bedabbled wretch
Turn, and return, indenting with the way;
Each envious briar his weary legs doth scratch,
Each shadow makes him stop, each murmer
stay:
For misery is trodden on by many,
And being low, never reliev'd by any.

—*Venus and Adonis,* ll. 703-08

Selecting a club for second shot

Can you nominate in order now the degrees of
the lie.

—*As You Like It,* V.iv

Self-critical pro

"So so" is good, very good, very excellent good; and yet it is not; it is but so so.

—*As You Like It,* V.i

Self-critical putter, after missing two-footer

Thou has most kindly hit it.

—*Romeo and Juliet,* II.iv

Senior tour veterans

If pleased themselves, others, they think,
delight
In such like circumstance, with such like sport:
Their copious stories, oftentimes begun,
End without audience, and are never done.

—*Venus and Adonis,* ll. 844-47

Sensitive to club pro's criticism of his swing

And will you credit this base drudge's words,
That speaks he knows not what?

—*King Henry VI, Part II,* IV.ii

Showboat teeing up on a long par 4

I will wink and hold out mine iron.

—*King Henry,* II.i

Skipping the Tour for a much-needed rest

But now I am cabin'd, cribb'd, confined,
bound in
To saucy doubts and fears.

—*Macbeth,* III.iv

Skittish woman golfer enters deep rough

Weaving spiders come not here,
Hence you long-legged spinners hence!
Beetles black, approach not near,
Worm not snail, do no offence.

—*A Midsummer Night's Dream,* II.ii

Small sympathy from club trainer

There be some sports are painful.

—*The Tempest,* III.i

SELF-SATISFIED GREENSKEEPER

How lush and lusty the grass looks! how green!

—*The Tempest,* II.i

Sorehead defaulter

Let's see the penalty. . . . Who devis'd this
penalty?

—*Love's Labour Lost,* I.i

Sour outlook on the top-ten list

They are as sick that surfeit with too much,
as they that starve with nothing.

—*The Merchant of Venice,* I.ii

Strange ball behavior

Hooking both right and wrong to th'appetite,
To follow as it draws!

—*Measure for Measure,* II.iv

Strong but erratic hitter

Over hill, over dale,
Thorough bush, thorough briar,
Over park, over pale,
I do wander every where.

—*A Midsummer Night's Dream,* II.i

Stuck in the amateur ranks

I am commanded here, and kept a coil with
"Too young," and "next year," and "'tis too
early."

—*All's Well That Ends Well,* II.i

Stymied

Lay out, lay out.

—*King Henry IV, Part I,* IV.ii

Sudden death playoff

This blow
Might be the be-all and end-all here.

—*Macbeth,* I.vi

Sure putter

I have a kind of alacrity in sinking.

—*The Merry Wives of Windsor,* III.v

Suspended club member

Sweet recreation barr'd, what doth ensue
But moody and dull melancholy?

—*The Comedy of Errors,* V.i

The swing is easy and the sound is right

True! pow, wow.

—*Coriolanus,* II.i

Taking a drop

The woods are ruthless, dreadful, deaf, and
dull.

—*Titus Andronicus,* II.i

Teaching pro's despair

That sport best pleases that does least know
how;
Where zeal strives to content, and the contents
Dies in the zeal of that which it presents.

—*Love's Labour's Lost,* V.ii

Teaching pros' methods

Such shapes, such gestures, and such sound,
expressing—
Although they want the use of tongue—a kind
Of excellent dumb discourse.

—*The Tempest,* III.iii

Tee shot rationalization

He does it with a better grace, but I do it more natural.

—*Twelfth Night,* II.iii

Texas Open

Fie! This is hot weather, gentlemen.

—*King Henry IV, Part II,* III.ii

That's not a gimme!

Play out the play.

—*King Henry IV, Part I,* II.iv

Third round leader

Doubt not of the day,
And that once gotten, doubt not of large pay.

—*King Henry VI, Part III,* IV.vii

Tied after 72 holes of tournament play

And when you breathe in your watering,
they cry
'hem!' and bid you 'Play it off!'

—*King Henry IV, Part I.* II.iv

Tiger Woods—I

I never knew so young a body with so old a
head.

—*The Merchant of Venice,* IV.i

Tiger Woods—II

He hath, indeed, better better'd expectation
than you
must expect of me to tell you how.

—*Much Ado About Nothing*, I.i

Tiger Woods considered favorite to win

This denoted a foregone conclusion.

—*Othello*, III.iii

Tiger Woods's endorsements

What piles of wealth he hath accumulated
To his own portion!

—*King Henry VIII*, III.ii

To lay up or not to lay up

If this should fail,
And that drift look through our bad
performance,
'Twere better not assay'd

—*Hamlet*, IV.vii

SHOT INTO THE GRANDSTAND AT AUGUSTA NATIONAL

Masters, spread yourselves.

—*A Midsummer Night's Dream,* I.ii

Tom Watson's chip-in at Pebble Beach, 1982 U.S. Open

Before my God, I might not this believe
Without the sensible and true avouch
Of mine own eyes.

—*Hamlet,* I.i

Too much club on second shot

Then, happy low, lie down!

—*King Henry IV, Part II,* III.i

Top ten money winners

The wealthy curled darlings of our nation.

—*Othello,* I.i

Tour hijinks

And therefore, living hence, did give ourself
To barbarous licence; as 'tis ever common
That men are merriest when they are from
home.

—*King Henry V,* I.ii

Tournament cut posting

I have heard better news.

—*King Henry IV, Part II,* II.i

Tournament galleries

What are these
So withered, and so wild in their attire,
That look not like th'inhabitants o'th'earth,
And yet are on't?

—*Macbeth,* I.iii

Tournament sponsors

Their love
Lies in their purses.

—*King Richard II,* II.ii

Tournament starter

I see you stand like greyhounds in the slips,
Straining upon the start.

—*King Henry V,* III.i

Triple bogey

O, horrible! O, horrible! most horrible!

—*Hamlet,* I.v

Trouble with short game

I am toiling in a pitch—pitch that defiles.

—*Love's Labour's Lost,* IV.iii

Two rounds in the same day

Never so weary, never so in woe;
Bedabbled with dew, and torn with briers;
I can no further crawl, no further go;
My legs can keep no pace with my desires.
—*A Midsummer Night's Dream,* III.ii

TV commentator

That tongue that tells the story of thy days,
Making lascivious comments on thy sport,
Cannot dispraise but in a kind of praise;
Naming thy name blesses an ill report.
—*Sonnet XCV*

Unable to recover from triple bogey

That one error
Fills him with faults; makes him run through all
th' sins.
—*The Two Gentlemen of Verona,* V.iv

Unconventional grip

By God's sonties, 'twill be a hard way to hit.
—*The Merchant of Venice,* II.ii

Unexpected royal invitation to an afternoon of golf

Why hath thy queen
Summon'd me hither, to this short-grassed
green?

—*The Tempest,* IV.i

Upon hearing that the clubhouse bar will reduce prices from four until seven

O most courageous day! O most happy hour!

—*A Midsummer Night's Dream,* IV.ii

U.S. Ryder Cup victory in 1999

It shall be raging mad, and silly mild,
Make the young old, the old become a child.

—*Venus and Adonis,* l. 1151-52

Veteran of the tour

How now! Which of your hips has the most
profound
sciatica?

—*Measure for Measure,* I.ii

Veteran pro's advice to newcomer on the Tour

Lay aside life-harming heaviness
And entertain a cheerful disposition.

—*King Richard II,* II.ii

Virtuous putter

His life is parallel'd
Even with the stroke and line of his great justice.

—*Measure for Measure,* IV.ii

Visiting royalty

This way, my lord, for this way lies the game.

—*King Henry VI, Part III,* IV.v

Wealthy sponsor to visiting pros

My purse, my person, my extremest means
Lie all unlock'd to your occasions.

—*The Merchant of Venice,* I.i

Well-guarded green

Here shall they make their ransom on the sand.

—*King Henry VI, Part II,* IV.i

ST. ANDREWS, SCOTLAND

Blow winds, and crack your cheeks! rage! blow!
You cataracts and hurricanes, spout.

—*King Lear,* III.ii

Well-hit second shot on a par 5 hole

But flies an eagle flight, bold, and forth on,
Leaving no tract behind.

—*Timon of Athens,* I.i

Well-hung golfer

His codpiece seems as massy as his club.

—*Much Ado About Nothing,* III.iii

"What do you think of my swing?"

Do not put me to't,
For I am nothing if not critical.

—*Othello,* II.i

Wind factor

The southern wind
Doth play the trumpet to his purposes;
And by his hollow whistling in the leaves
Foretells a tempest and a blustering day.

—*King Henry IV, Part I,* V.i

Winner by default

But I can give the loser leave to chide.

—*King Henry VI, Part II,* III.i

The yips—I

Feel, master, how I shake, look you, I
warrant you.

—*King Henry IV, Part II,* II.iv

The yips—II

How now, good fellow, why shakest thou so?

—*The Winter's Tale,* IV.iii

The Nineteenth Hole

Shakespeare borrowed all of his plots. Some critics contend that in this regard he lacked imagination. One thing can be said for his retold tales, however—they moved. Murder, rape, suicide, torture, lying, cheating, fornicating, mistaken identities, assumed identities, cross-dressing, and just about every other normal or abnormal human activity abound. Imagine if, like our postmodern masters, such as Beckett or Pinter, he had used his magnificent gift of language to suggest rather than elucidate, to befuddle rather than enlighten, or to communicate the failure of human communication, or to point out the pointlessness of life. He might very well have written a play about golf. Perhaps something like this...

WAITING FOR THE GREENSKEEPER

A golf course. The rough.

Enter TWO GOLFERS *and* CADDIE

FIRST GOLFER

Why upon this blasted heath you stop our way?

SECOND GOLFER [holding a golf ball]

Sometimes diverted these poor balls are ty'd
To the orb'd earth; sometimes they do extend
To view right on.

FIRST GOLFER

Praising what is lost
Makes the remembrance dear.

SECOND GOLFER

This even mead, that erst brought sweetly forth
The freckled cowslip, burnet, and green clover,
Wanting the scythe, all uncorrected, rank,
Conceives by idleness, and nothing teems
But hateful docks, rough thistles, kecksies, burs,
Losing both beauty and utility.

CADDIE

God be wi' you, an you talk in blank verse.

SECOND GOLFER

I must stand the course.

FIRST GOLFER

I will but look upon the hedge and follow you.

CADDIE

In each thing give him way, cross him in nothing.

FIRST GOLFER

Thou speakest wiser than thou art ware of.

CADDIE

I am a kind of burr; I shall stick.

SECOND GOLFER

A rascally yea-forsooth knave.

FIRST GOLFER

He wears the rose
Of youth upon him.

CADDIE [*Aside*]

Who would fardels bear,
To grunt and sweat under a weary life?

FIRST GOLFER [*Aside*]

The miserable have no other medicine
But only hope.

SECOND GOLFER

Leave thy vain bibble-babble.

CADDIE

Let the end try the man.

FIRST GOLFER

Away, you scullion! you rampalion! you fustilarian!

SECOND GOLFER

These are but wild and whirling words.

FIRST GOLFER

O! let me not be mad, not mad, sweet heaven,
Keep me in temper; I would not be mad!

CADDIE

Go hang yourselves all! you are idle shallow
things:
I am not of your element.

FIRST GOLFER

Get thee hence! Gone!

[*Exit* CADDIE]

FIRST GOLFER

I do begin to have bloody thoughts.

[*Enter* THIRD GOLFER]

THIRD GOLFER

Good dawining to thee, friend.

FIRST GOLFER

But who did bid thee join with us?

SECOND GOLFER

He needs not our mistrust, since he delivers
Our offices.

THIRD GOLFER

Present fears
Are less than horrible imaginings.

FIRST GOLFER

Do you bite your thumb at us, sir?

THIRD GOLFER

I do not bite my thumb at you sir; but I bite my thumb.

SECOND GOLFER

Though it be honest, it is never good
To bring bad news.

THIRD GOLFER

It will be rain to-night.

FIRST GOLFER

Let it come down.

SECOND GOLFER

The worst is not,
So long as we can say, "This is the worst."

FIRST GOLFER

Mine, and most of our fortunes, to-night shall be—drunk to bed.

THIRD GOLFER

I know a trick worth two of that.

[*Re-enter* CADDIE]

CADDIE

I grow, I prosper;
Now gods, stand up for bastards!

FIRST GOLFER

Home art gone and ta'en thy wages!

CADDIE

Present mirth hath present laughter;
What's to come is still unsure.

FIRST GOLFER

I am worse than e're I was.
And worse I may be yet.

THIRD GOLFER

I pray you, let none of your people stir me:
I have an exposition of sleep come upon me.

SECOND GOLFER

The posteriors of this day; which the rude multitude call the afternoon.

THIRD GOLFER

Thou hast the most unsavory similes.

SECOND GOLFER

Words, words, mere words, no matter from the heart.

CADDIE

More matter for a May morning.

THIRD CADDIE

Age, I do abohor thee, youth, I do adore thee.

FIRST GOLFER

Come, let us be gone.
Our revels now are ended.

SECOND GOLFER

The rest is silence.

[*Exeunt all*]